10/16

**Please check all items for damages
before leaving the Library.
Thereafter you will be held
responsible for all injuries
to items beyond reasonable wear.**

Helen M. Plum Memorial Library

Lombard, Illinois

A daily fine will be charged for
overdue materials.

FEB   2010

DOG HEROES®

COMBAT-WOUNDED DOGS

by Sunita Apte

Consultant: Janet Tobiassen Crosby, DVM

BEARPORT
PUBLISHING

New York, New York

Credits

Cover and Title Page, © U.S. Army photo by Staff Sgt. James Selesnick; Cover(RT), © U.S. Marines/ Lance Cpl. Geoffrey T. Campbell; Cover(RM), © U.S. Air Force/Staff Sgt. Lee Tucker; Cover(RB), © U.S. Air Force/Derek Kaufman; TOC, © Leigh S. Cann; 4, © AP Images/Jim MacMillan; 5, © Leigh S. Cann; 6, © Staff Sgt. Jacob N. Bailey/USAF; 7, © AP Images/U.S. Marines/Cpl. Miguel A. Carrasco Jr.; 8, © U.S. Marines/Lance Cpl. Geoffrey T. Campbell; 9, © U.S. Army/Staff Sgt. James Selesnick; 10, © Bettmann/Corbis; 11, © Topham/The Image Works; 12, © Reuters/USAF/Landov; 13, © U.S. Army/ Kenneth A. Robinson; 14, © U.S. Navy/Walter J. Pels; 15, © U.S. Air Force/Derek Kaufman; 16, © KRT/Newscom; 17, © AP Images/Eric Gay; 18, © AP Images/Eric Gay; 19, © U.S. Air Force/Robbin Cresswell; 20, © U.S. Air Force/Robbin Cresswell; 21, © AP Images/Eric Gay; 22, © AP Images/Lenny Ignelzi; 23, © U.S. Air Force/Staff Sgt. Lee Tucker; 24, © U.S. Air Force/Senior Airman Courtney Richardson; 25, © SHNS/Spc. Anna-Marie Hizer/U.S. Army/Newscom; 26, © AP Images/Walter Petruska; 27, © U.S. Navy/Petty Officer 2nd Class John F. Looney; 28, © U.S. Air Force/Staff Sgt. Stacy L. Pearsall; 29TL, ©Photodisc/Fotosearch; 29TR, © Arco Images/Alamy; 29BL, © Yann Arthus-Bertrand/Corbis.

Publisher: Kenn Goin
Senior Editor: Lisa Wiseman
Creative Director: Spencer Brinker
Design: Dawn Beard Creative
Photo Researcher: Amy Dunleavy

Library of Congress Cataloging-in-Publication Data

Apte, Sunita.
  Combat-wounded dogs / by Sunita Apte.
    p. cm. — (Dog heroes)
  Includes bibliographical references and index.
  ISBN-13: 978-1-59716-864-9 (library binding)
  ISBN-10: 1-59716-864-5 (library binding)
 1. Dogs— War use—United States—Juvenile literature. 2. Rescue dogs—United States—Juvenile literature. 3. Dogs—War use—United States—History—20th century—Juvenile literature. 4. Rescue dogs—United States—History—20th century—Juvenile literature. I. Title.
  UH100.A65 2010
  355.4'240973—dc22

                        2009011247

For more information, write to Bearport Publishing Company, Inc., 101 Fifth Avenue, Suite 6R, New York, New York 10003. Printed in the United States of America.

10 9 8 7 6 5 4 3 2 1

Table of Contents

Wounded!

It was January 2006. Soldier Brendan Poelaert and his **military** dog, Flapoor, were in the middle of **combat** in Iraq. Suddenly, a bomb exploded and the street beneath them shook! The blast was so strong that Brendan passed out from its force. When he woke up, his arm hung limp and broken by his side. Brendan wasn't interested in his arm, though. He was worried about Flapoor.

A street in Ramadi, Iraq, near where Brendan and Flapoor were in combat

When he finally spotted his dog, he saw that the powerful animal's chest was bleeding heavily. Brendan knew he had to get help, or Flapoor would die.

"I've got to get my dog to the **vet**!" he told the **medic** helping him.

Brendan Poelaert just minutes before the bomb exploded

Most military dogs are one of three **breeds**: German shepherd, Dutch shepherd, or Belgian Malinois, like Flapoor.

5

To the Rescue

The medic loaded Brendan and Flapoor into an SUV. Brendan pressed his fingers to the dog's chest to slow down the bleeding. He had to keep Flapoor alive!

As soon as they got back to the **base**, a veterinary medic took over. He put an **IV** into Flapoor. Then the dog was airlifted by helicopter to a hospital in Baghdad, Iraq's capital, for surgery.

The military uses helicopters to take wounded soldiers and dogs to nearby hospitals.

Luckily, Flapoor's operation was successful and he got over his injuries quickly. Brendan, however, took longer to heal. When both were healthy enough, the dog and soldier went home to the United States to fully recover.

Brendan Poelaert celebrates with Flapoor after receiving a medal for his bravery during the Iraq bombing.

Flapoor's injuries were caused by a piece of **shrapnel** that had pierced his lung.

Canine Soldiers

Today there are about 2,500 **canine** soldiers like Flapoor in the U.S. military. These dogs are known as military working dogs, or MWDs. They are stationed all around the world with many of them in Iraq and Afghanistan. These dogs, along with their **handlers**, have important jobs. Some help guard military bases. They search anyone who enters or leaves.

A soldier and his MWD patrol a street in Iraq.

Other dogs go off base to **patrol** and to search buildings and combat zones for enemy soldiers. Still others, called **detector dogs**, sniff for bombs with their powerful noses. These special MWDs can smell even tiny amounts of **explosives**. By finding bombs before they explode, the dogs save countless lives.

An MWD sniffs for weapons outside of a building in Iraq.

Currently, there are a couple hundred MWDs working in Iraq and Afghanistan. There are about another 2,000 dogs providing service at military bases in the United States and other places around the world.

A Long Military History

Although a few dogs were in combat during World War I (1914–1918), the United States officially began using these brave animals in World War II (1939–1945). The dogs worked on and off the battlefield. Some patrolled the coastlines. Others guarded soldiers, weapons, and buildings. The dogs were trained to attack and kill the enemy if ordered. They proved so helpful that the military used dogs again during the Korean War (1950–1953) and the Vietnam War (1957–1975).

Chips was one of the most famous military dogs in World War II. He received many medals for his bravery. There was even a TV movie made, called *Chips, the War Dog* (1990), based on his life.

Dogs played an especially useful role in Vietnam. Filled with thick jungles, it was hard for soldiers to see and hear. Due to their great sense of smell, sight, and hearing, the MWDs were perfect for scouting out the enemy and finding hidden weapons. It's estimated that these military dogs may have saved the lives of more than 10,000 soldiers.

An American soldier and his dog head for the jungle in Vietnam.

About 3,000 to 4,000 dogs served during the Vietnam War, many working through illness and injury.

From Equipment to Soldier

Until recently, the military viewed dogs as pieces of **equipment**, not as soldiers. Often, badly wounded dogs were put down, or gently killed, rather than given medical treatment. When dogs were sent to the war zone, no one made special plans to bring them back home. Most soldiers just left the dogs behind.

Nowadays, human soldiers and their MWDs often share a special friendship.

Today, things have greatly changed. The military realizes that well-trained war dogs are very valuable. They view these animals as four-legged soldiers. They're given the same kind of treatment as human soldiers. Wounded dogs get medical care, rest, and **rehabilitation**, or rehab. If a dog dies in the line of duty, a special funeral is held.

Britt, a retired military dog, was given a special military funeral when he died. Taps—the song used during funerals for soldiers—was played, and Britt's handler was presented with a flag.

MWDs usually have a higher military **rank** than their handlers. This encourages the handlers to treat their dogs well, since the animals are their superiors.

Dangerous Work

Military dogs have to deal with the same harsh conditions as soldiers. They suffer from many similar injuries, such as cuts and scrapes, in the line of duty. The hard work can also make them tired and ill.

In Iraq, the dogs can overheat in the blazing sun. Sand from the desert often irritates their eyes and ears. Many are stung by scorpions or bitten by spiders. Some are wounded by bullets or by glass and shrapnel from exploding bombs.

In Iraq, the temperature can get up to more than 100°F (38°C). Soldiers need to make sure that their four-legged partners drink plenty of water.

When serious injuries happen, trained army vets are ready to give aid on and off the battlefield. For example, an army vet in Iraq treated a wounded dog by putting in a **breathing tube** and performing surgery in the middle of the combat zone. The vet saved the dog's life.

Military dogs in Iraq have a lot of special safety equipment, including bulletproof vests and booties. Some dogs also wear Doggles, or doggie goggles, to protect their eyes from the desert sand.

Combat Dog Training

Since dogs have become such a valuable part of the military, a lot of time is spent training them. During a 120-day program at Lackland Air Force Base in San Antonio, Texas, these carefully chosen animals learn how to become MWDs.

As part of their training, the dogs learn how to obey their handlers, spot the enemy, and stay calm in crowds. They are also taught how to attack on command and sniff for bombs. When a dog performs well, he or she is rewarded with a toy and some playtime.

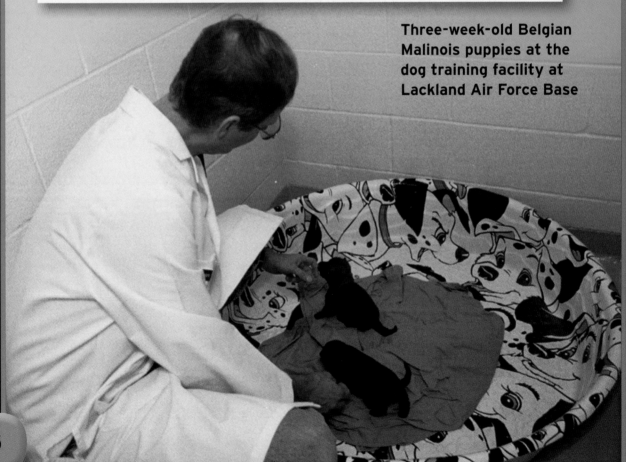

Three-week-old Belgian Malinois puppies at the dog training facility at Lackland Air Force Base

The dogs and their handlers spend a lot of time together, too. They learn how to work together as a team. It's important for them to look out for one another on and off the battlefield.

A dog handler works with a military dog during canine training at Lackland Air Force Base.

The dogs that enter the military training program are carefully chosen. They must be well behaved and have no health problems. Some of the dogs are bought from professional **breeders**. Others are bred on the base.

A Hospital Goes to the Dogs

Besides training, the Lackland center also treats injured and sick military dogs. For many years, hurt dogs were taken care of in an old hospital on the military base. However, the building was cramped and overcrowded. Vets weren't able to give the dogs the best care.

Some dogs at Lackland's new hospital get therapy on an underwater treadmill, which takes weight off their injured joints so they can excercise.

The military knew that something had to be done, so a new, larger hospital was built and opened in October 2008. This 30,000 square foot (2,787 sq m) facility offers all the care a badly wounded dog might need. There are two operating rooms, state-of-the-art testing equipment, and a special doggie gym for **physical therapy.**

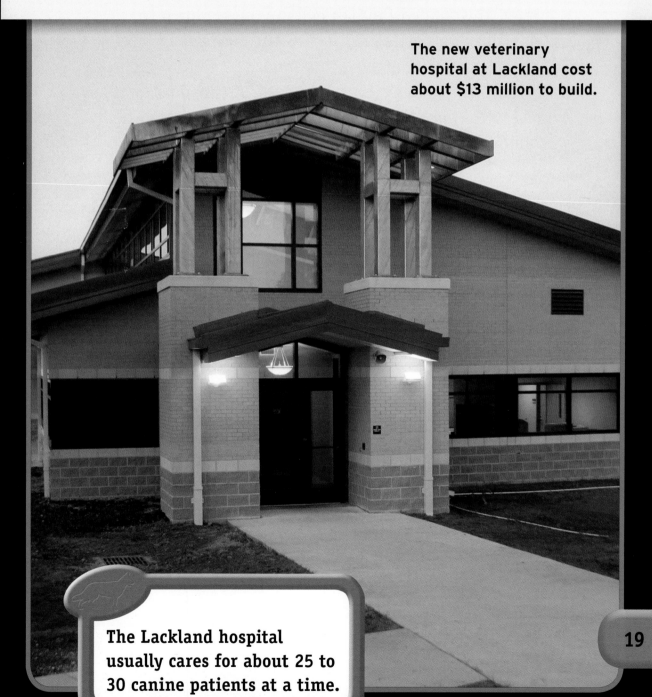

The new veterinary hospital at Lackland cost about $13 million to build.

The Lackland hospital usually cares for about 25 to 30 canine patients at a time.

The Process of Healing

Some dogs in the new Lackland hospital just need a little rest and rehab. Others need more help because they have serious physical injuries.

Buco, a wounded Belgian Malinois, was flown to Lackland from a battlefield in the **Middle East** in late 2008. When he first arrived, his hind legs were completely **paralyzed**. He couldn't even stand up. As hospital vets worked with him, Buco slowly improved. Eventually, he was able to stand and walk a few steps.

Dona, a military dog, receives treatment at the new hospital at Lackland.

Buco will stay at the hospital for as much time as he needs to heal. Then he will be either sent back into action or retired and put up for adoption. A law passed in 2000 allows some retired combat dogs to be adopted by their handlers or by the public.

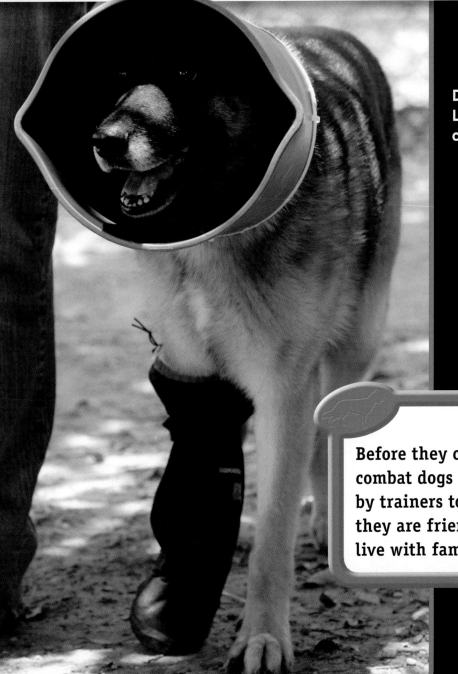

Dogs recovering at Lackland are well cared for.

Before they can be adopted, combat dogs are evaluated by trainers to make sure they are friendly enough to live with families.

Flown Out

When U.S. military dogs fall sick or are injured in another country, they receive immediate care on site. If the dogs need more intensive treatment, they are then flown to a hospital in Germany. Some are even brought to the hospital at Lackland. A dog that is too sick or injured to fly without medical care can be **aerovaced** to another hospital. During these flights, vets and medics offer the MWDs medical treatment in the air.

After soldier Megan Leavey and her dog were injured in Iraq, they were flown back to the United States for rest and rehab.

Ronny, a military dog, had to be aerovaced from the Middle East. His handler, Staff Sergeant Tim Cox, had noticed that Ronny seemed tired and "wasn't himself at all." An examination by the vet showed that Ronny had a problem with his heart and needed care that he could get only in Germany. On their flight, a vet traveled with them to care for Ronny along the way.

Staff Sergeant Cox carried Ronny onto the plane.

Military dogs are sometimes killed in action. Around ten dogs have been killed in combat in Iraq since the war began in 2003.

Doggie Doctors

There are more than 400 army vets working around the world. Whether in Iraq or Texas, these are the people responsible for making sure that military dogs stay in the best possible health.

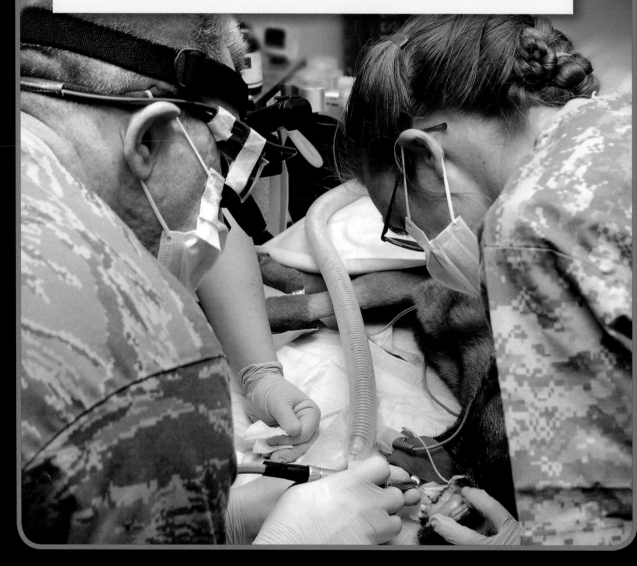

Military vets around the world not only perform check-ups and surgeries, but they can also do simple dental procedures.

On the **front lines** in Iraq, there is a group of army veterinarians at Forward Operating Base Warrior. These doctors run the base's animal clinic. They are responsible for the sick and injured dogs that come in from the battlefield.

Captain Kristie Souders is the doctor in charge. Her mission is to patch up injured dogs on the front lines and then, if necessary, give the order to fly them out to a larger hospital for more treatment.

Captain Kristie Souders says that one of the hardest parts of her job is saying good-bye to the dogs once it's time for them to leave. "Some of them I get attached to," she says. "It's hard to see them go."

Captain Kristie Souders (left) cleans a wound on an injured combat dog.

From Soldier to Pet

Like human soldiers, most military dogs are sent back into action after they heal. They usually work for about ten years. Dogs that have very serious injuries, however, are allowed to retire.

Sometimes a dog that has overcome an injury is allowed to retire, too. This was the case for a German shepherd named Lex, who was in Iraq with his handler, Corporal Dustin Lee. They were involved in an attack, and, sadly, Corporal Lee died. Although Lex was wounded, he survived and was healthy enough to be sent back to work. However, Corporal Lee's family wanted to adopt him. So Lex was given permission to retire early and live with Lee's family.

Lex, here with the Lee family, was the first military dog allowed to retire early in order to be adopted.

Lex still has shrapnel from the attack in his body.

Like Lex, many other four-legged soldiers fight bravely and are wounded in action. Hopefully, when their military service ends, they will all retire to loving homes.

Many states have put up memorial statues honoring combat dogs.

25 MARINE WAR DOGS GAVE THEIR
GUAM IN 1944. THEY SERVED AS SENTRIES
THEY EXPLORED CAVES, DETECTED MIN
SEMPER FIDELIS

KURT   YONNIE   KO
SKIPPER   PONCHO   T
NIG   PRINCE
MISSY   CAPPY
BLITZ   ARNO
BURSCH   PEPPER
TAM (BURIED AT   POINT)
GIVEN IN THEIR MEMORY AND O   THE SU
OF THE 2nd AND 3rd MARINE WAR   NS, MA
OWE THEIR LIVES TO THE BR   CRIFIC
GALLAN
BY WILLIAM W. PUTNE   PLATO
DEDICATED T   1994

Just the Facts

- Rags was a famous World War I military dog. He was found on the streets of Paris, France, and adopted by an American soldier. Rags was brought onto the battlefield, where he bravely carried messages through enemy lines. This heroic dog had his paw, ear, and eye damaged by shrapnel during battle. He also survived a gas attack.

- Antis was a World War II military dog that served with his Czech owner, Vaclav Bozdech, in the British Air Force. Antis was wounded several times, including once when he was shot in the face. After the war, in 1949, Antis was awarded a special medal for bravery.

- Perhaps one of the most famous U.S. military dogs in the Korean War was York. He successfully completed 148 combat patrols without any soldiers dying.

- Kaiser was the first U.S. Marine dog killed in the Vietnam War. Before he died, he saved the lives of many soldiers.

Common Breeds: MILITARY DOGS

German shepherd

Dutch shepherd

Belgian Malinois

aerovaced (*air*-oh-VAKT) flown on a special flight where medical treatment is given onboard

base (BAYSS) a safe center for military operations

breathing tube (BREE-thing TOOB) a tube that helps an injured person or animal breathe

breeders (BREE-durz) people who raise puppies

breeds (BREEDZ) types of animals

canine (KAY-nine) having to do with dogs

combat (KOM-bat) fighting

detector dogs (di-TEK-tur DAWGZ) dogs that can sniff out bombs

equipment (i-KWIP-muhnt) the tools and machines needed to do a job

explosives (ek-SPLOH-sivs) substances that can blow up

front lines (FRUHNT LINEZ) areas where battles take place in wars

handlers (HAND-lurs) people who help train or manage dogs

IV (EYE-VEE) a tube inserted into a person or animal's vein through which life-saving fluids, blood, and medicine can be given

medic (MED-ik) someone trained to give medical care

Middle East (MID-uhl EEST) an area made up of several countries, including Iraq and Saudi Arabia, that covers parts of Asia and Africa

military (MIL-uh-*ter*-ee) having to do with armies and war

paralyzed (PA-ruh-lized) unable to move parts of one's body

patrol (puh-TROHL) to walk around an area to protect it or keep watch on people

physical therapy (FIZ-uh-kuhl THER-uh-pee) the treatment of injuries through exercise, massage, and heat

rank (RANGK) an official position in the military

rehabilitation (*ree*-huh-*bil*-uh-TAY-shun) a process to restore one to good health

shrapnel (SHRAP-nuhl) small metal pieces from an exploded bomb

vet (VET) veterinarian; a doctor who takes care of animals

Bibliography

Hamer, Blythe. *Dogs at War.* London: Carlton Books (2001).

Karunanithy, David. *Dogs of War.* Hampshire, UK: Yarak Publishing (2008).

Lemish, Michael G. *War Dogs: A History of Loyalty and Heroism.* Dulles, VA: Brassey's (1999).

O'Donnell, John E. *None Came Home: The War Dogs of Vietnam.* Kearney, NJ: 1st Books Library (2001).

Read More

The American Kennel Club. *The Complete Dog Book for Kids.* New York: Hungry Minds, Inc (1996).

Mehus-Roe, Kristin. *Dogs for Kids: Everything You Need to Know About Dogs.* Irvine, CA: BowTie Press (2007).

Sanderson, Jeanette. *War Dog Heroes—True Stories of Dog Courage in Wartime.* New York: Scholastic Press (1997).

Learn More Online

Visit these web sites to learn more about combat-wounded dogs:

www.defenselink.mil/home/features/2006/working-dogs/index.html

www.lackland.af.mil/units/341stmwd/index.asp

Index

About the Author

Sunita Apte has written more than 40 books for children and teens. A dog lover, Sunita resides in Brooklyn, New York.